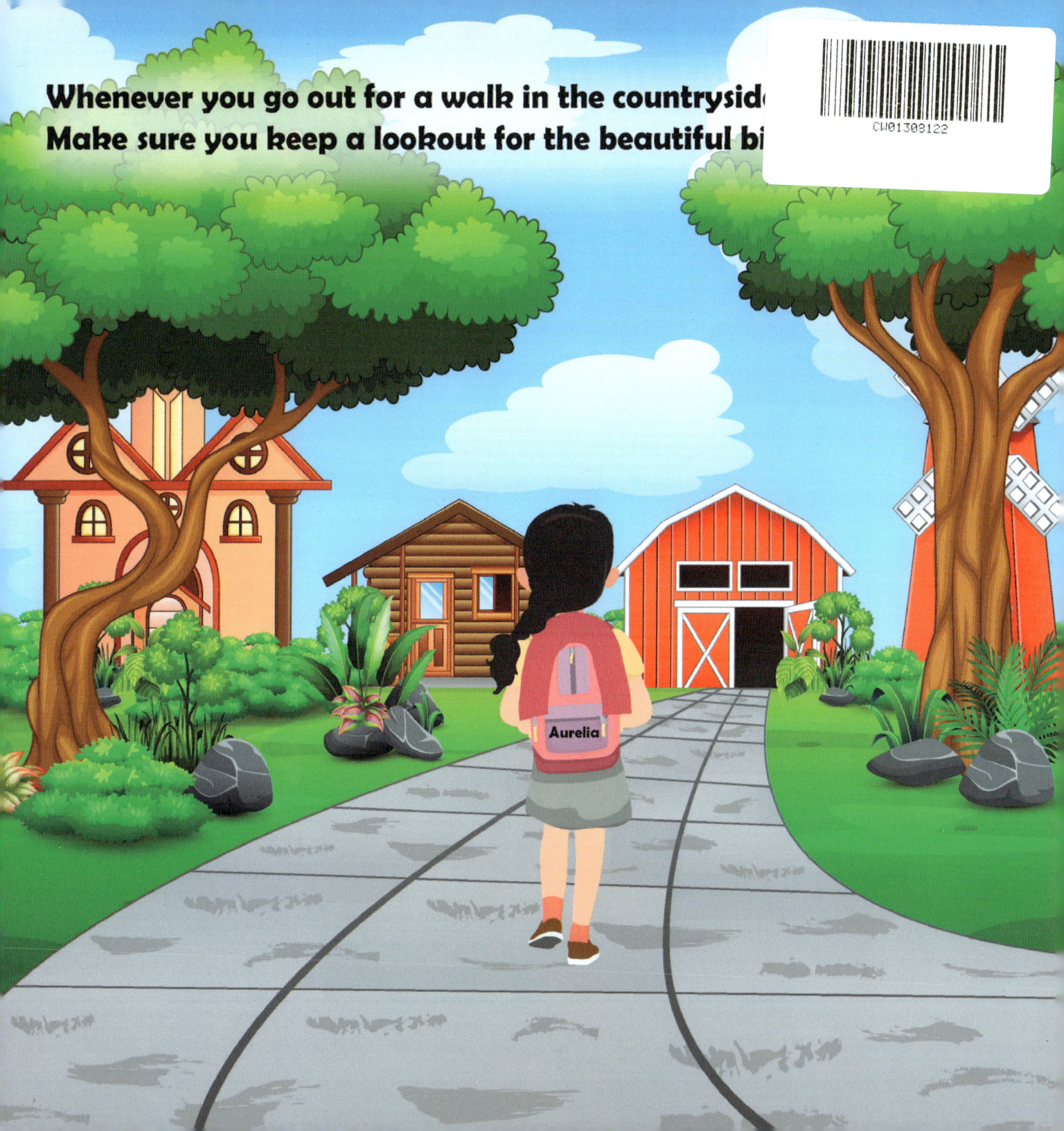

Whenever you go out for a walk in the countryside
Make sure you keep a lookout for the beautiful bi

We learn to recognise their songs and calls and watch them in their games.

Chirrup chirrup sparrows play in every tree we see.
Who's the first to spot one? Aurelia shouts out "Me!"

A nest with eggs means spring is here. How many will they lay?
But never touch or pick them up, you'll frighten mum away.

Tap- tap we hear in the forest, who can it possibly be?
A green and red woodpecker is making a hole in a tree.

Aurelia sits at the riverbank looking pretty in pink.
The dazzling kingfisher swoops down low and sips a lovely drink.

Speckled starlings flock together round and round they fly.
So many birds together make patterns in the sky.

The acrobatic blue tit is an easy bird to spot.
He loves the garden feeder and visits quite a lot.

Over fields the kestrel hovers and watches all around.
Then swooping down he moves so fast to catch his food upon the ground.

A family of ducks are swimming, neatly in a line.
How many babies are there? Aurelia can see nine.

Now she sees a graceful swan so elegant and white.
Her reflection in the water makes it such a wonderful sight.

Pigeons live so close to us in every street and town.
They watch us from the rooftops and make a cooing sound.

Bold and curious magpies are fun to watch at play.
They like to look for shiny things and steal them away.

The friendly robin sits nearby as Aurelia eats her lunch.
Worms are best he whistles, but he still likes to peck at the crumbs.

The melody of the blackbird tells us he's close by.
You can spot him by his black coat and pretty yellow eyes.

Seagulls love to ride the wind and soar across the sky.
But watch out if you are eating, they often want a try!

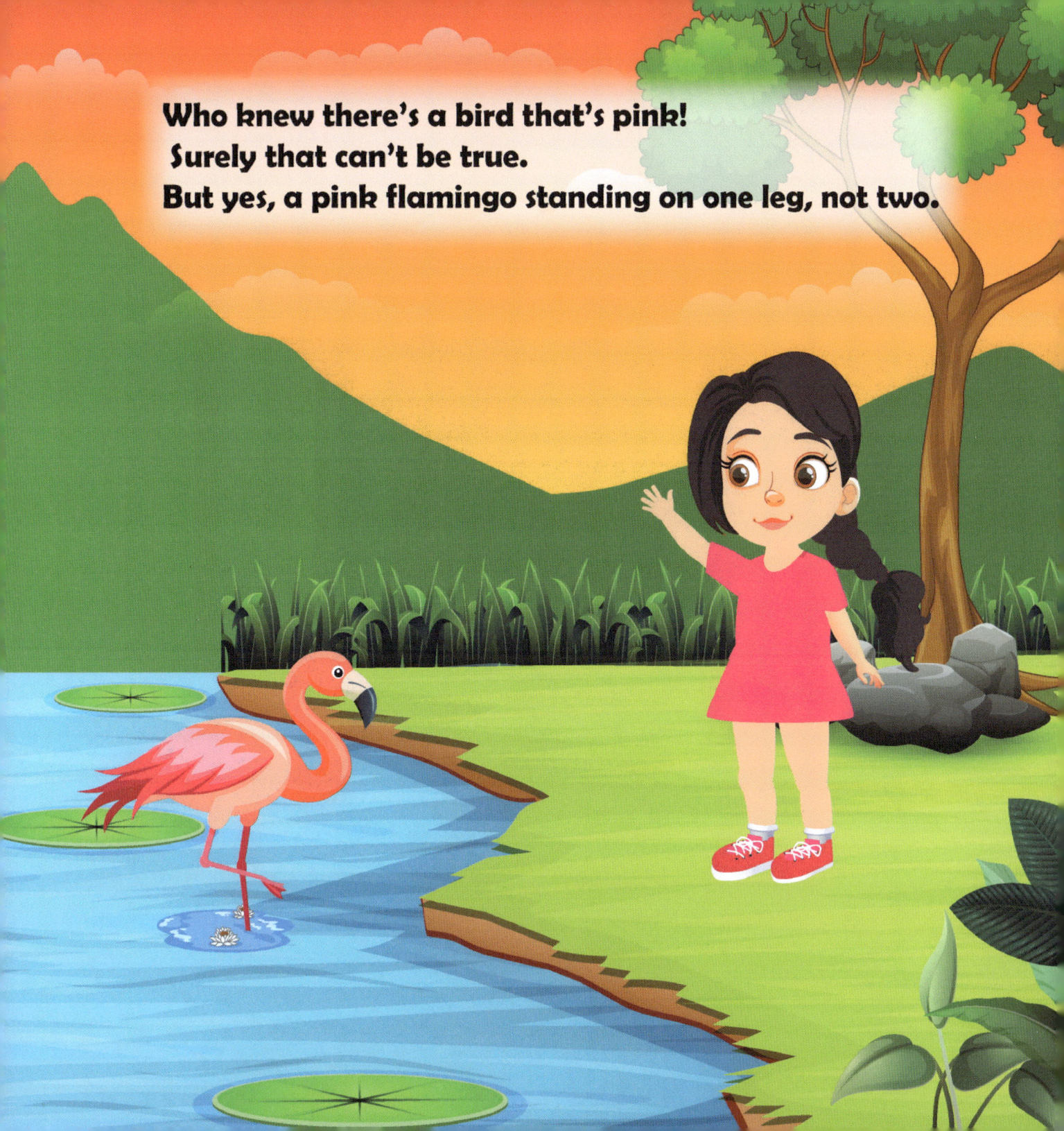

Who knew there's a bird that's pink!
Surely that can't be true.
But yes, a pink flamingo standing on one leg, not two.

**Tall and grey a heron stands as still as a statue of stone.
She waits and watches for the fish and always stands alone.**

Wow! The peacock shows his tail, green and violet and blue.
It looks as though a hundred eyes are staring back at you.

Puffins live along the coast, high up on the rocks.
Aurelia sails on a boat to take a better look.

We see the penguins at the zoo, sliding in ice and snow.
Aurelia thinks their walk is funny, waddling as they go.

A tiny bird we can't forget, the sweetest little wren.
She hides under the bushes then pops her head out again.

Day is turning into night, Aurelia hears "to whit to woo."
A big eyed owl looks around to hunt the whole night through.

**It's time for sleep, Aurelia's head is filled with all she's seen.
Her little bed is safe and warm and now it's time to dream.**

So many birds around us. It's fun to learn their names. How many can you remember?

- Blue tit
- Magpie
- Sparrow
- Swan
- Woodpecker
- Kingfisher
- Blackbird
- Robin

I wonder if the birds are watching us too?

**For my darling Aurelia.
Dream big little one.**

Printed in Great Britain
by Amazon